Crafting with Feminism

Crafting with Feminism

25 Girl-Powered Projects to Smash the Patriarchy

Bonnie Burton

QUIRK BOOKS

PHILADELPHIA

Library of Congress Cataloging in Publication Number: 2016930950

ISBN: 978-1-59474-927-8

Printed in China
Typeset in Franklin Gothic and Adobe Garamond

Designed by Andie Reid
Photographs by Liz Daly, except for the following pages by Mike Reali: 14, 17, 18, 20, 40, 42, 55, 61, 63, 64, 66, 80, 93, 102.
Production management by John J. McGurk

Quirk Books
215 Church Street
Philadelphia, PA 19106
quirkbooks.com

10 9 8 7 6 5 4 3 2 1

To my mom, step-mom, and grandmothers, Jane Wiedlin, Murphy Brown, Peppermint Patty, Princess Leia, Sarah Jane Smith, Buffy Summers, Uhura, and all the other feminists—fictional and real—who ever made me proud to be a girl with a wicked jaw.

TABLE CON

OF

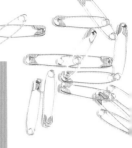

TENTS

FOREWORD by Felicia Day

Hi, my name is Felicia. I have a vagina and I make crafts.

In the past, when I had more free time, I would throw two or three crafting parties during the year. I'd invite all my lady friends over and offer them a buffet of glitter, pipe cleaners, construction paper, and stickers to create their perfect holiday greeting cards. Hosting my fellow females and giving them the chance to express their creativity through crafting was the ultimate get-together. I loved the look of concentration on the face of my lawyer friend, who hadn't made anything from scratch since high school, as she glued crooked ornaments to an awkward little Christmas tree. And the way my comedian friend snorted in laughter when she cut out a banana hammock for a Valentine's cupid.

The delight of making things by hand is something we need more of in our lives, and that's why I wholeheartedly love this book. Bonnie has taken many clichés about feminism and turned them into wonderful exercises of whimsy. The projects embody the spirit of optimism and determination that I associate with feminist activism—a spirit that, sadly, has fallen out of focus thanks to reactionary politics.

Recently, I was interviewed by a woman reporter, and she said to me, "I don't want to make you uncomfortable, and you don't have to answer if you want, but would you call yourself . . ." Her voice lowered to a whisper, like she was asking me something profane. ". . . a feminist?"

I was startled. I answered straightaway, "Yes, of course, I'm a feminist. I believe in equal rights between the sexes." But the incident lingered with me. Why did this woman act like she was asking me something dirty or embarrassing?

I believe that feminism is about giving women the freedom to make the choices they want to make and to be what they want to be. No one should be confined to a narrower list of options just because of the way she was born. Feminism has a million positive ideas that could drown out the negative—and a fun book like *Crafting with Feminism* is just what we need to help that cause along.

If you can get people to laugh about something loaded, you create space for them to think about things in a new light. And if you show that you don't take yourself seriously, you remind the rest of the world that we're all just trying to live as our authentic selves—even imperfectly. We're not much different from each other.

Think about this while you're making your sassy hoop art, feminist badge of honor, or cute little tampon buddy. I certainly will.

Besides crafts, actress and writer **FELICIA DAY** has created many things, including the hit Web series *The Guild*, the romance and fantasy book club Vaginal Fantasy, and the YouTube channel Geek & Sundry.

INTRODUCTION We Can Glue It!

It doesn't matter if you can knit socks with your eyes closed or if you struggle to sew a button on a shirt. As soon as you stick a pair of googly eyes on a boring salt shaker, you can call yourself a crafter.

Crafting is all about using creativity to transform ordinary materials into something greater than the sum of its parts. Just as anything can be a craft supply—pipe cleaners, felt pieces, old clothes, popsicle sticks, milk cartons, even rocks—anyone who picks up a glue gun can be a crafter. Learn the basics and you can make *anything*.

That DIY spirit isn't just a big part of the crafting revolution—it also keeps feminism alive and thriving (really!). That magical, powerful feeling you get from turning paper bags into puppets or transforming scraps of felt into stunning appliqués is the same spirit that has informed the feminist movement. Together we're stronger, cooler, and more awesome than we are on our own.

We know women are amazing—that's what makes us feminists! But, unfortunately, women all over the world struggle for equality. So what do we do when society tries to keep us down? We write, create art, sew clothes, start bands. We paint signs and protest. We express our frustrations and outrage by displaying them for the world to see.

In short, we make things happen by making things.

This craft book is meant to offer creative ideas for shouting out your opinions, pushing back on the haters, and paying tribute to your favorite female icons. From jewelry to home decor, these quirky DIY projects let you celebrate history's heroines, from the suffragettes who fought for the vote to second-wave feminists such as Gloria Steinem and Dorothy Pitman Hughes to riot grrrl bands like Bikini Kill.

But the best thing about this book isn't learning how to make projects with a feminist spin all by yourself; it's sharing the fun with all your friends. There's always room at the feminist crafting table for anyone who believes in equality, no matter their identity or ability—if you can cut, sew, glue, and have fun doing it, then this book is for you. With these projects, you can host crafty cocktail parties, get artsy with your book club, organize a DIY day for a fundraising project, or just hang out one-on-one while whipping up tributes to the pioneers and principles of feminism.

So grab a handful of glitter and get your girl power on. No one said feminism can't be fun!

Don't sit and wait for the opportunities to come. Get up and make them.

—Madam C. J. Walker

Projects

Feminist Badges of Honor

Girl Scouts earn a merit badge for everything from pet care to campsite cooking. Let's apply that can-do spirit to iconic feminist skills! Illustrate your prowess with fun icons, and then pin the badges anywhere you want to show off.

SUPPLIES

Paper and pencil

Dark pen

Cotton fabric

Felt

Shot glass or small drinking glass

Colored pencils or white chalk pencil

4-inch embroidery hoop

Embroidery needle and floss

Scissors

Pinback fasteners or safety pins

Straight pins

Sewing needle and thread (optional)

Fabric pencil

Fabric glue

Glitter, glitter glue, or sequins (optional)

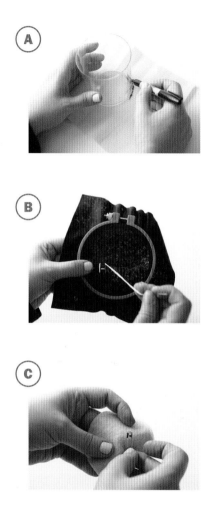

INSTRUCTIONS

1 Sketch design ideas or use our suggestions (opposite). The simpler the design, the easier it will be to embroider. Use a dark pen to draw the final design on a fresh piece of paper.

2 Place the shot glass (for a larger badge, use a drinking glass) on the fabric. Use a pencil to trace around the base of the glass (A), but don't cut out the circle.

3 Next, use a pencil or pen to trace around the top of the same glass onto a contrasting color of felt.

4 Transfer the design from step 1 onto the smaller fabric circle. If the fabric is light, place it directly on top of the paper and trace the design with colored pencil (using pencil in the same color as your thread will help hide the lines). If the fabric is dark, use a white chalk pencil to redraw the design on the fabric.

5 Place the fabric inside the embroidery hoop and stretch it taut, positioning the design in the middle. Thread a large embroidery needle with 3 strands of floss in the color of your choice and tie a small knot at one end. Starting from the underside of the fabric, sew along the lines of your design using small, straight stitches (B). When done with each color of floss, tie another knot on the underside of the fabric. Trim floss.

6 Cut out both the embroidered front circle and felt back circle. Sew or glue the pinback fastener or safety pin to the felt circle (C). Attach the embroidered front circle to the felt circle by applying fabric glue around the edges, or by pinning it in place with straight pins and sewing around the edges with either sewing thread or embroidery floss.

7 For extra sparkle, glue or sew on sequins, or pipe glitter glue around the edges. Let dry if needed, and then wear with pride.

MERIT BADGE IDEAS

Total Babe	I ❤ Me
Zine Queen	Riots Not Diets
No Scale Award	Girls Rule
Body Pos	Feelin' Myself

Heroes of Feminism Finger Puppets

Heroes like Frida Kahlo, bell hooks, and Ruth Bader Ginsburg might come from different walks of life, but all are strong women who made a mark in their field and paved the way for the rest of us to follow in their footsteps. What better way than a handy puppet to honor these icons.

SUPPLIES

Images of your favorite feminist icons from the Web to use as a guide for your puppets' hairstyles and clothes

Paper and pencil

Finger puppet template (page 21)

Felt in various colors (body, clothing, accessories, etc.)

Straight pins

Scissors

Pipe cleaners

Sewing needle and thread (in colors matching your felt)

Fabric glue

Fabric

Embroidery floss

Small googly eyes

Yarn (for hair)

Fake fur (optional)

INSTRUCTIONS

1 Trace or photocopy the finger puppet template on page 21 onto a piece of paper. Cut out pattern. Fold the felt for the body in half and attach the paper pattern using straight pins (A). Cut out the pattern, creating two body pieces. Repeat with head and hand pieces.

2 Make a face: Separate 3 strands of embroidery floss and use them to thread the needle. Sew a few stitches onto the head piece to make a nose and mouth, or cut out a mouth from red felt and affix with fabric glue. (Save the googly eyes for later!)

3 Cut the pipe cleaner into two small pieces the length of the puppet's arm. Place the cut pipe cleaners on one of the two body pieces as shown (B) and glue in place. This will make the arms of your puppet bendable.

4 With needle and thread, sew together the two body pieces using a straight stitch, leaving the bottom open. Glue or sew the hands to the arms and the head to the neck.

5 Using the printed image of your feminist as a guide, give your puppet hair, wardrobe, and accessories. For hair, glue or sew on unraveled yarn, embroidery thread, or fake fur. For clothes, use the puppet as a template and cut out garments from felt or fabric scraps. Glue or stitch any clothing pieces together and dress your puppet (or glue or sew the clothes directly on the puppet). Finish by gluing on googly eyes or tiny black beads.

Heroes of Feminism
Finger Puppets
template

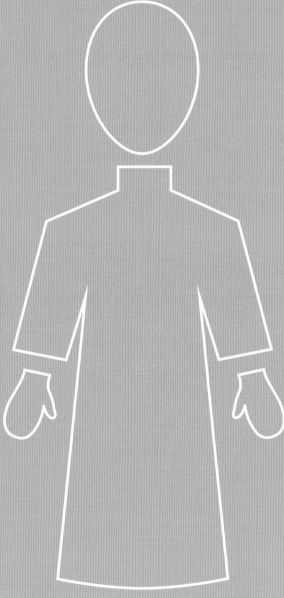

Pizza Not Patriarchy Reusable Lunch Bag

Feminists believe their food can serve a purpose in spreading the word. Beyond carrying tasty fuel, this reusable and washable lunch bag looks like a monster slice of pizza and displays a bold feminist slogan.

SUPPLIES

Paper and pencil

Scissors, X-Acto knife, or rotary cutter

Ruler

½ yard of yellow oilcloth or laminated cotton

Duct tape in brown (for crust), red, green, and silver (for toppings)

Large sewing needle and heavy-duty polyester thread

Thimble (optional)

Adhesive hook-and-loop dots

Vinyl letter stickers

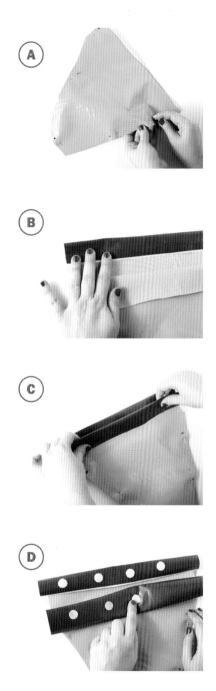

INSTRUCTIONS

1 Make a pattern: On the paper, draw a large triangle, about 13 inches long along the edges of the "slice" and 9 inches across on the "crust" side. Cut out the triangle.

2 Fold the oilcloth in half and tape the triangle pattern to the front. Using the scissors, X-Acto knife and ruler, or rotary cutter, cut triangle from the fabric (you should have two separate triangles). Stack the triangles, shiny side out, and pin together (A).

3 For the crust, cut a piece of brown duct tape as long as the top of the triangle. Stick the tape to the top of one of the pinned triangles and fold it over (B) to form a crustlike edge. Repeat at the top edge of the other triangle (C).

4 Sew the long edges of the triangles together using needle and heavy-duty thread (or a sewing machine, if you prefer), leaving the crust edge open. (The fabric can be tough, so use a thimble to protect yourself from accidental jabs!)

5 Stick or sew hook-and-loop dots to the inside of the crust (D). These will allow you to fasten the bag.

6 Now for the toppings! Cut out mushroom shapes from the silver duct tape, pepperoni circles from the red duct tape, and thin strips of bell peppers from the green duct tape. Adhere vinyl letters to spell out PIZZA NOT PATRIARCHY in the middle of the bag, then stick the topping shapes all around.

7 Fill the bag with your lunch, snacks, or a slice of pizza.

ROCKIN' FEMINIST PLAYLIST

Get your groove on while you stitch and glue with these classic girl-power anthems.

1. **REBEL GIRL**
Bikini Kill

2. **CHERRY BOMB**
The Runaways

3. **RUN THE WORLD (GIRLS)**
Beyoncé

4. **THESE BOOTS ARE MADE FOR WALKIN**
Nancy Sinatra

5. **CAN'T HOLD US DOWN**
Christina Aguilera and Lil' Kim

6. **TYPICAL GIRLS**
The Slits

7. **TALKIN' BOUT A REVOLUTION**
Tracy Chapman

8. **NOT A PRETTY GIRL**
Ani DiFranco

9. **IT'S A NEW FIND**
Shonen Knife

10. **NO SCRUBS**
TLC

11. **GIRLS! GIRLS! GIRLS!**
Liz Phair

12. **ONE WAY OR ANOTHER**
Blondie

13. **NONE OF YOUR BUSINESS**
Salt-n-Pepa

14. **RESPECT**
Aretha Franklin

15. **WHIP MY HAIR**
Willow

16. **ARMY OF ME**
Björk

17. **Q.U.E.E.N.**
Janelle Monáe, feat. Erykah Badu

18. **PROUD**
Tegan and Sara

19. **GIANTS**
Kimya Dawson

20. **JUST A GIRL**
No Doubt

21. **YOU OUGHTA KNOW**
Alanis Morissette

22. **BITCH**
Meredith Brooks

23. **BAD GIRLS**
M.I.A.

24. **BORN THIS WAY**
Lady Gaga

25. **GIRL ON FIRE**
Alicia Keys

26. **DANCING ON MY OWN**
Robyn

All Hail the Queen Crown

Too many fairy tales involve a charming prince saving a young damsel from a life of toil and trouble just by marrying her and resting a bejeweled crown upon her head. Here in the real world, you know better. All you need to feel like a queen is flexible cardboard, fabric, lace, felt, fake flowers, and—of course—glitter. No royalty required.

SUPPLIES

To make a cardboard crown:

Measuring tape or long piece of yarn

Paper and pencil

Thin cardboard (from a cereal box or cardboard mailing envelope)

Scissors

Stapler

Felt

Hot-glue gun

Acrylic paint and paintbrushes

Sparkly fabric

Fake flowers

Fake gemstones

To make a lace crown:

Polyester-blend lace (ideally with a wide bottom strip and a tall, ornate design on the top)

Fabric stiffener and a disposable container or glass bowl

Paintbrushes

Aluminum foil or wax paper

Acrylic paint

Mod Podge

Glitter (or sprayable glitter paint)

Sprayable clear acrylic coating

INSTRUCTIONS

For a cardboard crown:

1 Use the measuring tape or yarn to measure the diameter of your head. Cut out a piece of cardboard slightly longer so that it will wrap around your head with the ends overlapping (A). (It's okay if the cardboard needs to be in two pieces—just staple or glue the ends together after decorating it in step 3 to make a circle that fits your head.)

2 Cut a strip of felt or cardboard identical to the base of the crown. Hot-glue it to the inside of the crown's base to reinforce the crown.

3 Paint the outside of the crown with your favorite color acrylic paint, or hot-glue sparkly fabric all over to cover. Decorate the crown using fake flowers, fake gems, or other adornments. Let dry.

4 Hot-glue the ends of the base together. Let dry.

For a lace crown:

1 Cut a piece of lace long enough to wrap around your head.

2 Pour a bit of fabric stiffener into the disposable container. Using a paintbrush, apply stiffener to both sides of the lace to fully saturate (the more the better!). Be sure no clumps of stiffener block the holes in the lace design.

3 Place the saturated lace on foil or wax paper. Let dry.

4 Paint both sides of the stiff lace with acrylic paint (B). Let dry.

5 With a paintbrush, apply Mod Podge to one side of the lace and then sprinkle a layer of glitter on top. Let dry. Repeat on the other side. (Alternatively, skip the Mod Podge and glitter altogether and use glitter spraypaint instead.) Let dry.

6 Hot-glue the ends together.

7 To help keep glitter in place, spray the crown with clear acrylic coating. (Glitter has a habit of getting *everywhere*, so expect some extra bling in your hair when you wear this sparkly tiara.) Let dry.

> Fabric stiffener is a craft medium used for textile projects that pretty much does what you'd expect: keeps fabric stiff and molded. Find it at craft and fabric stores and online. For this project, be sure to get the paint-on kind in a bottle, not the spray-on kind in a can.

Tampon Buddies

Who says menstrual products have to be embarrassing? With a few simple supplies and a little imagination, you can transform a boring tampon into a delightful little friend.

SUPPLIES

Tampons

Scissors

Embroidery needle and floss

Fabric scraps

Felt scraps

Pipe cleaners

Hot-glue gun

Googly eyes

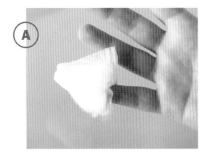

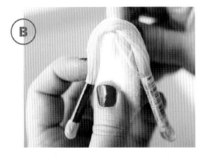

INSTRUCTIONS

1 Remove and recycle the applicator of one tampon. Cut off the string.

2 Push a finger inside the tampon, molding the material around your finger to give it a nice fluffy shape (A).

3 Make the doll's hair: Thread a needle with 3 strands of embroidery floss from a full skein. Lay the remaining skein of embroidery floss over top of the tampon (B). Sew in place with floss down the "part line" (C).

4 For the doll's clothes, wrap the base of the tampon with fabric scraps and sew or glue in place.

5 For the face, hot-glue googly eyes and felt scraps to the front of the doll.

TIP: To make an animal tampon buddy (as shown at right in photo on page 30), use one fluffed-out tampon for the body. For the head, hot-glue a cotton ball to the top of the tampon. Decorate with pipe cleaners for limbs, scraps of felt for ears, and googly eyes.

I am not afraid. I was born to do this.

—Joan of Arc

Drinking Dames Flask

Decoupage a portable bottle with images of your fave cocktail-lovin' gals and you'll never drink alone. Take inspiration from Dorothy Parker, Mae West, Nora Charles, and even the iconic absinthe green fairy.

SUPPLIES

Liquor flask

Patterned decorative paper, such as scrapbooking or origami paper

Scissors

Mod Podge

Clear varnish (optional, see tip on page 36)

Paintbrush

Cut-out pictures of famous feminists drinking

INSTRUCTIONS

1 Cut a long piece of decorative paper tall enough to cover the flask and a little more than twice as long as the flask is wide (A). (Or cut two pieces, one for the front of the flask and one for the back.)

2 With a paintbrush, apply Mod Podge or varnish to one side of the paper. (This will help make the surface resistant to moisture in case of spills.) Let dry. Repeat on the other side of the paper.

> **TIP:** Clear varnish will give your flask a shiny finish, but you can apply more Mod Podge to the exterior if you'd like.

3 Brush the surface of the flask with Mod Podge or varnish and then wrap the paper around the flask, smoothing wrinkles as you go. Add a bit more Mod Podge under the free end of the paper and firmly press onto flask to secure. Let dry.

4 Brush Mod Podge to the back of the cut-out images and press onto flask. Let dry.

5 Cover all decorated parts of the flask with another coat of Mod Podge, and let dry. Then drink up!

Search the Internet for images of your favorite drinking dames or pick up vintage postcards and advertisements that feature girls raising a glass.

Queen Ring Bling

Famous royal feminists who called the shots were known for their bravery and their bling. Pay homage to Nefertiti, Cleopatra, Anne Boleyn, Queen Elizabeth, and other lady leaders by sporting rings adorned with their images.

SUPPLIES

Small (less than ½ inch square) printed photos of famous queens

Stiff white paper and pencil

Flat glass marbles (used in flower arranging)

Scissors

Mod Podge, paintbrush, and paper plate

Craft glue

Blank metal ring bases (used in jewelry making, available at craft stores and online)

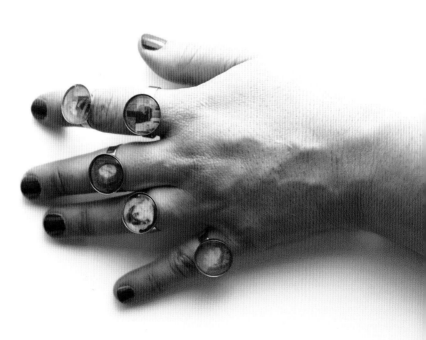

INSTRUCTIONS

1 For each ring, cut out the image of a queen and use craft glue to affix it to the white paper. (This will make the image more vibrant and opaque in the ring.)

2 Place a flat marble over the picture and trace around the edge. Cut out the image to be the same size and shape as the flat side of the marble.

3 With a paintbrush, apply Mod Podge to the flat side of the marble. Press the flat side of marble onto the top of the cut-out image. (The Mod Podge will dry clear.) Let dry. Trim any extra paper that sticks out from under the flat side of the marble.

4 Apply a small amount of craft glue to the flat part of the ring backing and press the flat side of the marble onto the glue. Hold the ring and marble together between your fingertips for about a minute, and then let dry completely for an hour or two. Slip it on your finger and wear it with pride.

Look up images of famous queens: Boudicca, Cleopatra, Nefertiti, Mary Queen of Scots, Catherine the Great, Victoria, Elizabeth (I and II!), Rani Lakshmibai, Tzu-hsi, Hatshepsut.

CRAFTERNOON PARTY INSPIRATION

Throw a bash for all your crafty feminist friends (see page 83 for party planning tips). Below are some theme ideas.

Like a Fish Needs a Bicycle Party

Male Chauvinist Tears Coffee Mug (page 91)
Pizza Not Patriarchy Lunch Bag (page 23)
Nope Necklace (page 55)

Decorate Your Space Party

Em-broad-ery Hoop Art (page 49)
Food for Thought Plates (page 95)
High Heels Are a Pain Planters (page 73)

Women's History Party

Heroes of Feminism Finger Puppets (page 19)
Queen Ring Bling (page 37)
Grrrl Coat of Arms Banner (page 99)

Bad-Ass Bridal Shower

All Hail the Queen Crown (page 27)
Drinking Dames Flask (page 35)
Feminist Killjoy Sash (page 61)

Underneath It All Party

Secret Stash in Your Rack (page 77)
Power Panties (page 45)
Burning Bra (page 65)

Feminist Baby Shower

Next-Gen Feminist Onesie (page 85)
Peace and Equali-tea Aromatherapy Candles (page 69)
Vagina Tree Ornaments (page 59)

Huggable Uterus Body Pillow

Being a strong woman is hard when menstrual cramps make you want to stay in bed all day. So when the crimson tide rolls in, hug this uterus-shaped pillow made of comfy fleece and you're sure to feel better. There's even a pocket to slip in a heating pad.

SUPPLIES

For the uterus pillow:

Simple image of a uterus (from a textbook or online search)

Large sheet of paper or newspaper and pen

Scissors

2 yards each of white, dark pink, and light pink fleece fabric

Straight pins

Sewing needle and thread to match fabric

Adhesive hook-and-loop fastener dots

2 pounds poly pillow stuffing

Chopstick

Black felt and fabric glue (for face, optional)

For the microwaveable heating pad:

Terry cloth washcloth

Sewing needle and thread

2–3 cups uncooked rice

2 ounces (about 1 cup) dried lavender (available at natural foods stores and online)

Bowl and spoon

Plastic funnel

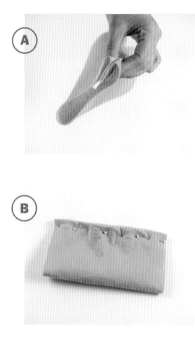

A

B

INSTRUCTIONS

To make the uterus pillow:

1 Make a uterus pattern: Fold both the uterus image and the sheet of paper in half lengthwise. Using the small image of the uterus as a guide, draw a larger half-uterus shape (at least 16 inches tall) onto the paper. Cut out the pattern and unfold it.

> **TIP:** After unfolding, you should have a single symmetrical uterus shape. You can also draw your pattern freehand, without a picture: the basic shape of a uterus is like a fat capital letter T.

2 Fold the piece of light pink fleece in half. Pin the unfolded uterus pattern onto the folded fleece. Cut around the edge of the pattern to create two identical uterus shapes for the front and back of the pillow.

3 Make the pocket: cut a piece of pink fleece big enough to hold your heating pad (about 6 inches by 8 inches). Fold the fleece in half lengthwise, then fold the top edges under and in by about 1 inch (A). Pin top edges together (B) and sew along top edge, leaving the sides open. Attach the hook-and-loop dots on the insides of the two pocket openings (this will keep the heating pad secure when inside the pocket), then place pocket in the center of one of the uterus pieces and pin in place along top sewn edge. Sew top edge of pocket to uterus piece.

4 Pin together the front and back uterus pieces, making sure the pocket is on the inside (you'll sew the pieces and then turn the pillow inside out to hide the seams). With matching thread, sew almost completely around the edges of the uterus, leaving an opening large enough for stuffing. Turn pillow inside out and stuff with poly stuffing, using the chopstick to push filling into the corners. Sew pillow closed.

5 For the Fallopian tubes, cut out two pairs of rectangles about 20 inches by 5 inches from dark pink fleece. Trim one edge of each rectangle with diagonal cuts to create three fingerlike ends (these will attach to the ovaries in step 6). Pin together each pair and sew with matching thread along three of the four edges, leaving one short edge open. Turn inside out, fill with poly stuffing, and sew closed. Sew the straight end of the tubes onto either side of the uterus.

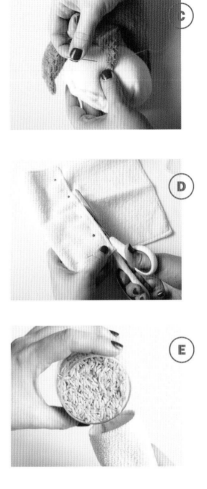

6 For the ovaries, cut out two pairs of circles from the white felt. Pin together each pair and sew together with matching thread, leaving an opening for stuffing. Turn inside out and fill with poly stuffing. Sew ovaries closed, and then sew one to the zigzag end of each Fallopian tube (C).

7 For a more cartoonish pillow, cut white felt circles for eyes, black circles for pupils, and a black felt curve for a smile. Sew or glue onto the front of the pillow.

To make a microwaveable heating pad:

1 Fold one end of the washcloth to form a pouch (D). Sew together along the long side and one short side (but not both) to form a tube. Turn inside out so seams are on the inside.

2 Combine rice and lavender in a bowl. Use the funnel to pour the rice mixture into the terry cloth tube until it's full but not over-stuffed (it should feel like a firm beanbag) (E). Sew closed.

3 To use, microwave heating pad on high power for up to two minutes and then carefully tuck into the pocket. Hug tight where needed.

This homemade heating pad is scented with soothing lavender. You can stuff your pillow with an ordinary hot water bottle if you prefer.

Power Panties

Wearing your feminism on your sleeve is always welcome, but why not try displaying it somewhere a little more… personal? Wickedly wise messages give a powerful update to boring old days-of-the-week knickers. Be sure to wash these daring drawers by hand, instead of in the washing machine, to extend their life.

SUPPLIES

Cotton underwear (in white, black, and various colors)

For the snazzy sequins method:

Washable fabric pen

Sewing needle and thread

Sequins (use strands for straight letters or loose sequins for curved/cursive lettering)

For the fabric sticker method:

Felt letter stickers

Sewing needle and thread

For the bleach pen method:

Bleach pen

Cardboard

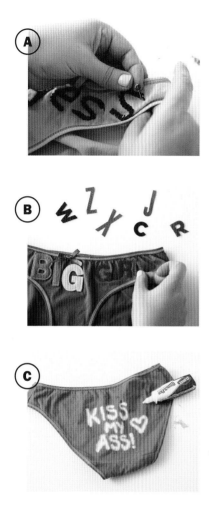

INSTRUCTIONS

You can inscribe your skivvies in several ways.

Snazzy sequin method

Use a washable fabric pen to write slogans on the underwear. Thread sewing needle with thread that matches the underpants fabric. If your letters are straight, lay strands of sequins over letters and attach to fabric with straight pins. Use a matching thread to sew in place.

If your lettering is curvy, use loose sequins: bring the needle up from the inside of the fabric, string on a sequin, then take the needle back down through the fabric at the edge of the sequin (so that one side of the sequin is stitched in place). Bring needle up again through fabric at the edge of the sequin, string on a second sequin, and repeat until slogan is covered (A).

Felt letter sticker method (B)

Before removing the backing from the letters, place them on undies to ensure that your message looks the way you want. Remove backing and adhere letters. Next, thread a sewing needle with thread and sew straight stitches along the edges of the letters to secure.

Bleach pen method (C)

This technique works best on dark-colored or black underwear. Place a piece of cardboard inside the underwear so that the bleach doesn't bleed through to the other side. Use a bleach pen to write the slogan directly onto the fabric.

POWER PANTIES SLOGAN IDEAS

Feminism Is Sexy

Big Girl Panties

Inner Goddess

My Body, Myself

Em-broad-ery Hoop Art

Needlework has long been considered a dainty art for well-behaved women, but we think it could use a 21st-century update. Bring some fresh 'tude to homespun wisdom with these fun and fierce wall hangings.

SUPPLIES

Colorful patterned fabric (½ yard per 8-inch hoop)

Self-adhesive felt letters

Ruler and fabric chalk (optional)

8-inch embroidery hoop

Scissors

Embroidery floss and needle

INSTRUCTIONS

1 Attach self-adhesive letters to fabric to spell out the saying of your choice. (For maximum precision, use a ruler and fabric chalk to draw straight lines, attach letters on the lines, and then gently brush away the chalk.)

2 Place fabric in the embroidery hoop, positioning the slogan in the center. Pull fabric taut and firmly secure hoop.

3 Separate 3 strands of embroidery floss. Use them to thread the embroidery needle, then knot one end. Starting from the underside of the fabric, poke the needle through so that it comes up on the side of the first letter in your saying. Take a big stitch over the letter and bring the needle down on the other side of the letter, so that the thread wraps over the letter's surface. Bring the needle up again just underneath your first stitch, and repeat this stitch process to cover the whole surface of the letter in long stitches (A).

4 When you've finished with one color of floss, secure the thread on the back of the fabric: bring the needle to the back of the hoop (B), then slide the needle through previous stitches and pull thread so it is caught underneath your stitchwork. Trim excess thread, then rethread needle with a different color and repeat steps 3 and 4 to cover remaining letters.

5 Trim excess fabric around the hoop. Display proudly.

FIERCE HOOP ART SLOGANS

Females Are Strong as Hell

Bitches Get Things Done

Whatevz

Go Away

Women Belong in the House...and the Senate

FEMINIST HOLIDAYS

Need an excuse to celebrate? Pick one of these woman-centric special days:

JOAN OF ARC'S BIRTHDAY
January 6

GLITTER DAY
Second Saturday of January

ROSA PARKS DAY
February 4 (her birthday) or December 1 (day of her famous arrest)

GALENTINE'S DAY
February 13

INTERNATIONAL WOMEN'S DAY
March 8

RUTH BADER GINSBURG'S BIRTHDAY
March 15

MAYA ANGELOU'S BIRTHDAY
April 4

THARGELIA, FESTIVAL OF THE GODDESS ARTEMIS
May 6

ANNIVERSARY OF SOJOURNER TRUTH'S "AIN'T I A WOMAN?" SPEECH
May 28 and 29

INTERNATIONAL YARNBOMBING DAY
June 11

ANNIVERSARY OF VALENTINA TERESHKOVA'S MISSION AS FIRST WOMAN IN SPACE
June 16

HELEN KELLER'S BIRTHDAY
June 27

NATIONAL SISTERS' DAY (U.S.)
August 7

WOMEN'S EQUALITY DAY
August 26

CELEBRATE BISEXUALITY DAY
September 23

ADA LOVELACE DAY
Mid-October (varies year to year, check Google for this year's date)

ANNIVERSARY OF THE MILLION WOMAN MARCH
October 25

JANE AUSTEN'S BIRTHDAY
December 16

Superheroine Wrist Cuffs

Everyone wants to be a superheroine on occasion. Now you can look the part with these impressive wrist cuffs that even an Amazon princess would be proud to wear. (Just don't use them to try to deflect speeding bullets.)

SUPPLIES

Cardboard tubes from paper towels
 or toilet paper

Scissors

Felt

Hot-glue gun

Glitter foam sheets

Glitter foam star stickers

Handheld hole punch

Ribbon

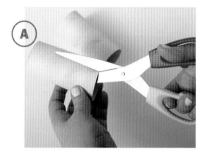

INSTRUCTIONS

1 Trim cardboard tubes to cuff length. Cut a vertical slit in each tubes so you can slip them onto your wrists (A).

2 Using the cardboard cuffs as a template, cut felt rectangles to fit inside cuffs (B). Hot-glue felt inside cuffs.

3 Cut glitter foam rectangles to fit over the outside of the cuffs and hot-glue in place. Hot-glue glitter foam stars to outside of cuffs.

4 Punch holes in both ends of the cuffs. Cut two 10-inch lengths of ribbon, thread through holes, and tie cuffs onto wrists. Now go save the world!

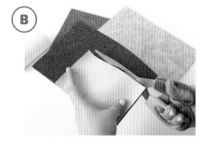

Nope Necklace

Sticking up for yourself by saying "no" is a powerful feminist act. Wear this necklace as a reminder that no matter what society expects, you don't always have to acquiesce.

SUPPLIES

For Scrabble tile method:

Epoxy glue (such as E6000)

N, O, P, and E Scrabble tiles

Necklace with simple, wide pendant

Binder clips

For letter bead method:

N, O, P, and E letter beads

Embroidery floss (for bracelet) and/or necklace chain

Small split rings (available at jewelry supply stores and online) and needle-nose pliers (for necklace)

For ransom note method:

Cut-out N, O, P, and E letters from a magazine or newspaper

Thin cardboard (from a cereal box)

Craft glue or Mod Podge

Scissors

Necklace chain

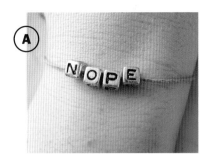

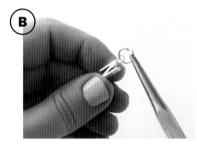

INSTRUCTIONS

Scrabble tile method

1 With epoxy glue, attach tiles together by their edges so that they spell the word NOPE (see page 55). Let dry.

2 Use epoxy glue to attach NOPE design to the front of the necklace pendant. Hold in place with binder clips. Let dry.

Letter bead method

1 For a bracelet, cut a length of embroidery floss to fit around your wrist. Thread on N, O, P, and E beads (A).

2 For a necklace, use needle-nose pliers to attach split rings to N, O, P, and E hanging beads (B). Thread rings onto necklace chain.

Ransom note method

1 Arrange cut-out letters to spell NOPE on top of thin cardboard. Glue (or Mod Podge) in place and let dry.

2 Cut out NOPE pendant from cardboard. Glue NOPE pendant to chain opposite clasp (C).

MUST-WATCH FEMINIST FILMS

Forget "chick flicks"—play an empowering movie in the background as you craft and chat with your gal pals.

ADVANCED STYLE
(dir. Lina Plioplyte, 2014)

This colorful documentary bursts at the seams with style as it follows well-dressed older women who don't let their age stop them from looking fabulous.

BELLE
(dir. Amma Asante, 2013)

Gugu Mbatha-Raw stars as Dido Elizabeth Belle, the illegitimate mixed-race daughter of the first Earl of Mansfield, in this based-on-a-true-story period drama about a woman of color fighting for equality and finding love in British society.

BEND IT LIKE BECKHAM
(dir. Gurinder Chadha, 2002)

Friendship, football, and fun: this hilarious story of Jesminder "Jess" Bhamra (Parminder Nagra), an 18-year-old Punjabi Sikh woman determined to play soccer despite her family's objections, has it all.

BUT I'M A CHEERLEADER
(dir. Jamie Babbit, 1999)

The now-classic satirical comedy tells the story of, yes, a cheerleader (Natasha Lyonne) who's sent to undergo conversion therapy to "cure" her lesbianism.

THE COLOR PURPLE
(dir. Steven Spielberg, 1985)

Based on Alice Walker's Pulitzer Prize–winning novel, this Academy Award–nominated film about the struggles of African American women—and the friendship that sustains them—stars Whoopi Goldberg, Oprah Winfrey, and Margaret Avery.

CLUELESS
(dir. Amy Heckerling, 1995)

Um, as if! Alicia Silverstone stars as socially savvy Beverly Hills teen Cher Horowitz in this cult classic comedy loosely based on Jane Austen's *Emma*.

FRIED GREEN TOMATOES
(dir. Jon Avnet, 1991)

Female friendship—both in the era of the Depression and the "modern" 1980s—is at the heart of this acclaimed film starring Kathy Bates, Jessica Tandy, Mary Stuart Masterson, and Mary-Louise Parker as two generations of strong Alabama women.

KIKI'S DELIVERY SERVICE
(dir. Hayao Miyazaki, 1989)

This delightful animated tale of a young witch learning her trade and finding herself in a new city is a charming (and kid-friendly!) alternative to clichéd cartoon princess movies.

NINE TO FIVE
(dir. Colin Higgins, 1980)

This timeless, Bechdel-test-busting buddy comedy features the unstoppable trio of Lily Tomlin, Jane Fonda, and Dolly Parton as coworkers who resort to desperate measures to rid their office of a sexist boss.

PERSEPOLIS
(dir. Marjane Satrapi and Vincent Paronnaud, 2007)

Based on Satrapi's graphic memoir of the same title, this animated film chronicles the author's life and coming of age among her Persian family in the time of the Iranian Revolution.

REAL WOMEN HAVE CURVES
(dir. Patricia Cardoso, 2002)

America Ferrera stars as Ana García, a hardworking Mexican American girl who dreams of going to college, in this uplifting (and body-positive) tale of self-acceptance and family.

WE ARE THE BEST!
(dir. Lukas Moodysson, 2013)

Outcast teens Bobo, Klara, and Hedvig team up to start an all-girl punk band in this energetic and joyful Swedish film about rocking out and being yourself in spite of the haters.

Vagina Tree Ornaments

Decorate your holiday tree—or everyday houseplants—with these festive lady-centric ornaments made from homemade salt dough. Create a variety of shapes and sizes, paint them all different colors, and glitter them up for an extra-glam vag!

SUPPLIES

4 cups flour

1 cup salt

2 cups water

Pink gel food coloring (optional)

Mixing bowl and wooden spoon

Rolling pin or empty wine bottle

Oval cookie cutters of different sizes, or a sharp knife

Cookie sheet

Toothpicks

Oven

Acrylic paint in various colors

Paintbrushes

Glitter

Sprayable clear acrylic coating

Ribbon or embroidery floss

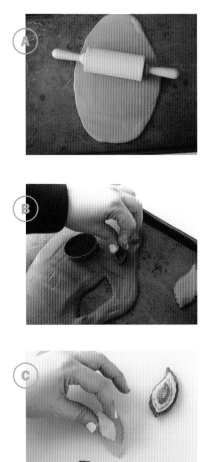

INSTRUCTIONS

1 In a mixing bowl, stir together the flour and salt. Then slowly stir in water, along with a few squeezes of pink gel food coloring if desired. Knead mixture with your hands until it has the consistency of cookie dough.

2 Using the rolling pin, roll out the dough on a floured work surface until it's about ¼ inch thick (A).

3 Use the cookie cutters or knife to cut out a few ovals in different sizes (B). Fold each smaller oval lightly in half and press or mold together until they resemble the lips of the vulva. Press each vulva into one of the larger ovals (C).

4 Using a toothpick, poke a hole at the top of each dough vagina so you can hang the ornament after it's baked. Place dough vaginas on a cookie sheet. Repeat steps 2–4 with remaining dough.

5 Bake for an hour, or until ornaments are hard. Remove from oven and let cool completely.

6 Paint as desired with acrylic paint. Add glitter, spray on clear acrylic coating, and let dry.

7 Thread ribbon or floss through the hole of each ornament and knot into a loop. Hang on your tree or anywhere you need a feminine touch.

Feminist Killjoy Sash

Tired of being called a party pooper every time you mention equal pay or sexism in gaming? Turn that insult on its head and wear it with pride on a decorative sash.

SUPPLIES

At least 6 feet of wide satin ribbon (enough to drape comfortably across your body)

Satin trim in a contrasting color (or black)

Scissors

Straight pins

Sewing needle and thread to match ribbon

Large iron-on letters

Iron

INSTRUCTIONS

1 Drape the satin ribbon over one shoulder to determine the length you need; trim to length. Cut 2 strips of satin trim the same length as the ribbon.

2 Pin the satin trim to either side of the wide ribbon. Sew in place with needle and thread.

3 Cut out iron-on letters spelling the slogan of your choice and place them along the ribbon. Affix letters with straight pins and then try on the sash to make sure they're positioned where you want them. Iron the letters onto the ribbon according to package instructions.

4 Pin the ends of the ribbon together using straight pins and then sew ends together (A). Now your sash is ready to wear!

SASS FOR YOUR SASH

Miss Behaves

Most Likely to Rebel

Queen of Everything

Future Mrs. Nobody

Burning Bra

Legend has it that members of the women's liberation movement burned their bras to protest sexism at the 1969 Miss America pageant. Although the story is apocryphal, these activists did launch a movement against stereotypes holding them back in an era when women could be denied loans, jobs, and housing, just for being ladies. Add to the mythos by adorning your undergarment with hot flame appliqués—no fire needed!

SUPPLIES

A favorite bra

Pencil and paper

Scissors

½ yard of red or orange cotton fabric

Embroidery hoop

Red, orange, and yellow sequins (loose or in strands)

Emboidery needle and red, orange, and yellow embroidery floss

Craft glue (optional)

Liquid seam sealant, such as Fray Check (optional)

Straight pins

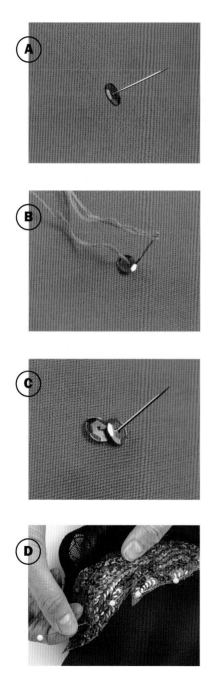

INSTRUCTIONS

1 Make a flame template: Use a pencil to sketch a flame shape on the paper, matching the bottom edge to the underside of your bra cup. The entire flame shape should fit within the embroidery hoop. Cut out the template.

2 Place template on cotton fabric. Use a pencil to trace the flame shape onto fabric.

3 Place fabric in the embroidery hoop with the flame shape in the center. Stretch fabric taut and secure it in the hoop.

4 Attach sequins: begin with your darkest color along the outside edge of the flame. Thread the needle with 3 strands of embroidery floss in a matching color and knot the end. Bringing the needle up from the underside of the hoop, thread a sequin onto the needle (A) and pull thread taut, holding the sequin in place against the fabric. Bring the needle down on the outside of the sequin (B) and pull taut, securing sequin in place. Bring needle back up on the outside of the attached sequin and thread a second sequin onto the needle (C). Holding second sequin in place, pull thread taut, then secure as with first sequin. Repeat, creating a line of sequins, until the flame shape is filled.

TIP: You can use strands of sequins to cut down on sewing time. Pin each strand in place along flame shape and sew to secure, or cut appropriate lengths and affix with craft glue.

5 Repeat steps 1–4 to create a second appliqué, making sure that the flame curves in the opposite direction (for the other side of bra).

6 Being careful not to snip the sequin threads, cut out flame appliqués. (Optional: apply liquid seam sealant around the edges of the flame to prevent wayward threads and let dry.) Pin one appliqué to each bra cup (D) and sew in place with matching thread.

I would not waste my life in friction when it could be turned into momentum.

—Frances Willard

Peace and Equali-tea Aromatherapy Candles

Self-care is an important part of activism. Effecting change is important work, but if you don't take breaks once in a while you're bound to get stressed. Do yourself a favor and relax with these calming scented candles nicely nestled inside upcycled teacups.

SUPPLIES

Vintage teacups with matching saucers (browse flea markets or antiques stores)

Wooden chopsticks

Prewaxed candle wicks

Clear tape

Shallow saucepan or frying pan with tall sides

Large, heatproof glass measuring cup with a spout (such as Pyrex)

1½ pounds candle wax flakes (4–6 ounces per candle)

Candle dyes

Scented essential oils, such as rose or jasmine

Oven mitts

INSTRUCTIONS

1 Lay 2 chopsticks side by side on top of the teacup. Thread a wick between them so that the metal base of the wick rests in the middle of the cup's bottom and the top pokes through the chopsticks (A). Tape the ends of the chopsticks together so that they hold the top of the wick in place. Repeat for as many candles as you wish to make.

2 Make a double boiler to melt the wax flakes: Fill a saucepan with water to an inch below the rim and place on the stove over medium heat. Place the heatproof measuring cup inside the pan and pour wax flakes into the cup (B). Maintaining a simmer, stir the melting wax flakes with a chopstick and add candle dye and scented oil—a couple drops of each. Be sure to stir the mixture so the scent spreads evenly throughout the candle.

3 Once the wax has melted completely, remove the pan from heat. Using oven mitts, carefully lift measuring cup out of the pan.

4 Pour liquid wax slowly into each teacup, leaving ¼ to ½ inch of space at the top (C).

5 When all the candles are filled, immediately wash measuring cup before wax residue cools and hardens. Let candles set. (This might take a few hours.)

6 Once the wax is opaque and firm, trim the excess wick at the chopsticks. Remove tape and chopsticks.

7 Place teacup candle on a pretty matching saucer. Light candle. Relax.

You can find candle-making supplies at many craft and hobby stores, but the Internet is best for variety and selection. Pick up ecofriendly options whenever possible so that your candles won't release yucky stuff into the air.

High Heels Are a Pain Planters

Wearing high-heeled shoes can be sheer torture. When you can no longer bear to wear them, upcycle these painful fashion accessories into sculptural pots for succulents and cacti.

SUPPLIES

A retired pair of high heels

Colorful electrical tape

Hammer and nail

Heavy-duty gardening gloves

Gravel

Potting soil

Small cactus, succulents, or air plants

Plastic or glass plates or dishes

INSTRUCTIONS

1 Cut small strips of electrical tape and use them to line the inside of the shoes. This will help waterproof the inside.

2 Turn shoes upside down. Using the hammer and nail, carefully puncture the sole of the toe box to create drainage holes (A).

3 Wearing gloves, place a layer of gravel inside the toe box of each shoe. Add soil to fill the toe box.

4 Use fingers to make a hole in the soil big enough for the plant, then carefully transfer the plant to the shoe (B). Place each planter on a plate to protect surfaces.

Look for heels that have a fairly large toe box to give your plant plenty of space. For obvious reasons, avoid peep-toes, slingbacks, and any styles with holes.

RECOMMENDED READING

New to feminism, crafting, or both? Crack open one of these classics to learn up fast:

TITLE **BAD FEMINIST**

AUTHOR **ROXANE GAY**

Critic and novelist Roxane Gay explores a range of feminism-related topics from pop culture to sexual politics in this best-selling series of essays.

TITLE **CRAFTIVISM**

AUTHOR **BETSY GREER**

From revolutionary ceramics to yarn bombing and beyond, this comprehensive history of crafting for social change is a great resource for any DIYer who wants to make a difference with her work.

TITLE **HOW TO SUPPRESS WOMEN'S WRITING**

AUTHOR **JOANNA RUSS**

This bitingly sarcastic "guidebook" takes a witty and disarming look at the various forces that conspire to oppress or erase writing by women.

TITLE **OUR BODIES, OURSELVES**

AUTHOR **OUR BODIES OURSELVES**
(FORMERLY BOSTON WOMEN'S HEALTH BOOK COLLECTIVE)

A radical sensation when it was first published in 1971, this classic guide to women's physical health was revised and updated in 2011 to add topics like gender identity and activism to its chapters on sexual health, childbearing, menopause, and other medical issues.

TITLE **FEMINISM IS FOR EVERYBODY: PASSIONATE POLITICS**

AUTHOR **BELL HOOKS**

The title speaks for itself! This author (whose lowercase nom de plume is an homage to her maternal grandmother) has written many excellent and thoughtful works in the feminist canon, addressing issues like the historic marginalization of black women and the intersections between racism, sexism, and class.

TITLE **KNITTING YARNS: WRITERS ON KNITTING**

EDITOR **ANN HOOD**

In this collection of first-person essays, beloved writers like Sue Grafton, Barbara Kingsolver, and Ann Patchett talk about the power and delight of working with two needles and a ball of yarn.

TITLE **THE FEMININE MYSTIQUE**

AUTHOR **BETTY FRIEDAN**

This groundbreaking 1963 book dug deep into the myths and mores of the midcentury housewife and is widely credited with setting the second wave of feminism in motion.

TITLE **THE SUBVERSIVE STITCH: EMBROIDERY AND THE MAKING OF THE FEMININE**

AUTHOR **ROZSIKA PARKER**

This fascinating history of needlework explores how the traditionally feminine craft of embroidery has run parallel to—and even shaped—the history of Western women.

TITLE **WE SHOULD ALL BE FEMINISTS**

AUTHOR **CHIMAMANDA NGOZI ADICHIE**

Nigerian author Adichie puts forth her views on twenty-first-century feminism in this excellent book-length essay—you may recognize it from Beyoncé's 2013 hit "Flawless"!

TITLE **WOMEN'S WORK: THE FIRST 20,000 YEARS: WOMEN, CLOTH, AND SOCIETY IN EARLY TIMES**

AUTHOR **ELIZABETH WAYLAND BARBER**

For thousands of years, textile production was done by hand—and by women. This fascinating history book reveals how influential those crafty women were in shaping the fabric (get it?) of civilization.

Secret Stash in Your Rack

Anyone who's shopped for women's clothing knows the frustration of falling in love with the perfect dress or skirt and quickly discovering it doesn't have any pockets. Until fashion designers give us the storage space we deserve, you can keep your cash and credit cards safe in this hidey-hole tucked into your bra.

SUPPLIES

Paper and pencil

½ yard of satin fabric

Straight pins

Iron and ironing board (optional)

Sewing needle and thread

Adhesive hook-and-loop fastener dots

A favorite bra

INSTRUCTIONS

1 Photocopy or trace the pocket template on page 79 onto a piece of paper. Cut out shape.

2 Pin pattern to satin fabric and cut out. Set pattern aside.

3 Make the pocket: Fold edges of cut satin shape in by ¼ inch on all sides and pin in place. Fold pinned satin in half, with the triangular point at the top, to form a pocket (A). Secure with additional pins. Sew pocket sides together, then continue sewing around edges of top flap to secure folded-over hem in place. You should have an envelopelike pocket with a hemmed top flap.

> **TIP:** Using an iron to press down the folded satin will help it stay in place before you pin.

4 Make the strap: Cut a small rectangle (approximately 2 inches by 5 inches) out of satin. Fold the rectangle in half lengthwise and pin together the long edge and one short edge with straight pins. Sew the pinned edges, leaving the other short edge open. Remove pins and turn rectangle inside out through open short edge, so that the seams are hidden. Sew remaining short edge closed.

5 Attach the strap to the pocket: Affix one end of strap to inside of pouch flap with straight pins. Sew in place as shown so that strap extends from pointed edge of flap (B).

6 Using your bra as a guide, affix fastener dots to outside of pocket and inner top edge of loop strip so that the pouch sits between bra cups when fastened (C). Tuck in your cards and cash, and your stash is complete.

Secret Stash
in Your Rack
template

Monster Week Tampon/Pad Case

Feel like a monster during menstruation? Make a tampon or pad case to match your mood. It won't prevent cramps or premenstrual syndrome, but at least it can make you smile.

SUPPLIES

½ yard of fake fur in a bold color

Straight pins

Sewing needle and thread

Felt in different colors

Small pom-poms

Googly eyes

Fabric glue

Adhesive hook-and-loop fastener dots

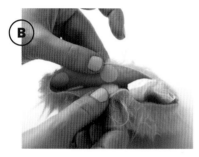

INSTRUCTIONS

1 Measure two squares or rectangles of fake fur big enough to hold the menstrual product of your choice.

2 Pin together fur rectangles with furry sides facing out. Sew closed on three sides, leaving the top open.

3 Give your pouch a face: Cut a mouth and teeth from felt. Use fabric glue to affix mouth, teeth, pom-pom nose, and googly eyes (A).

4 Affix fastener dots to the inside of the bag's open edge (B).

5 Place tampons or pads inside until needed.

PLAN THE PERFECT CRAFTERNOON

Nothing's more fun than crafting with friends. Here's how to throw a great get-together:

1 Pick projects.

Anything in this book will work (obviously!), but be sure to pick a craft that's appropriate for the skill levels of all your guests. (See page 39 for theme ideas.) If you choose a craft with a substantial amount of hands-off time (for drying/cooling/baking, etc.), be sure to plan an activity for while you wait (maybe pop in one of the movies on page 57!)

2 Shop for supplies.

Even if you're asking guests to BYO part of the craft (say, a mug to decorate), the host (that's you!) should be the one handing out all the stuff. When in doubt, buy more than you think you'll need—someone might screw up and need to start over (and besides, you can never have too many sequins!).

3 Prep your space.

Stay ahead of sticky stains by laying newspaper over your workspace (secure with painter's tape). Offer guests old shirts to wear as smocks.

4 Feed your friends.

No crafternoon is complete without snacks! Go the classy-lady route with tiny sandwiches and tea, or indulge in an antidiet smorgasbord of chips, cookies, and candy. If drinking's your thing, wine, beer, or cocktails will liven things up. Just be sure to keep your craft supplies and your snack spread separate— you don't want someone sipping the paint water by mistake!

5 Craft away!

Read the instructions first—all the way through— and make sure everyone understands them. More experienced crafters can help newbies by demonstrating techniques, too. If someone messes up, no big deal—imperfection's all part of the game. (And you thought ahead and bought enough supplies so they can start over!)

6 Share your stuff.

When everyone's finished, snap a picture of each crafter with her creation. Everyone can upload them to social media for immediate humblebragging, or you (as the host) can order prints of the pics (many photo sites offer a postcard option) and send them out to your guests as thank-yous. Either way, make memories!

Next-Gen Feminist Onesie

Until our budding feminists can talk, we can let their clothing do it for them. This cuddly onesie makes a great shower gift or birthday present for the little ones in your life.

SUPPLIES

Cotton onesie

Medium-size iron-on letters,
   medium-size adhesive felt letters,
   or nontoxic puffy fabric paint

Scissors

Iron (for iron-on letters)

Needle and thread

Pencil

INSTRUCTIONS

1 Lay onesie on a flat surface. If using iron-on letters, cut out letters and arrange them into a slogan (come up with your own or use one of ours, below). Affix each one to onesie using an iron according to package directions.

2 If using adhesive felt letters, arrange letters into a slogan, peel off backing, and adhere each one to the onesie. Then stitch in place using small, straight stitches.

3 If using fabric paint, use a pencil to sketch a slogan onto the onesie. Then paint over the pencil lines, adding decorative dots or swirls if you're feeling artsy. To keep design vibrant, hand wash onesie inside-out in cold water.

NEXT-GEN FEMINIST SLOGANS

Future Feminist

My Mom Breastfeeds

This Princess Saves Herself

Your Sexism Makes Me Cry

This Onesie Is Gender Neutral

I became a feminist as an alternative to becoming a masochist.

—Sally Kempton

Girl Band Cassette Business Card Holder

Cassettes are the perfect size for storing business cards. Search garage sales and flea markets for examples from famous women in pop music, like the Go-Go's, Madonna, the Supremes, Shonen Knife, the Runaways, L7, Bikini Kill, and Sleater-Kinney.

SUPPLIES

Cassette of a famous and feisty girl band

Small screwdriver

X-Acto knife

Pliers

Clear electrical tape

½-inch self-adhesive magnets
 (or smaller, if you can find them)

Craft glue

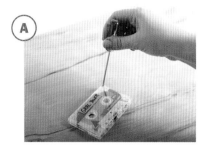

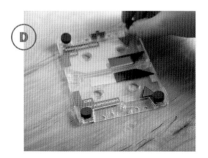

INSTRUCTIONS

1 Use the screwdriver to unscrew the two sides of the cassette (A). If the cassette doesn't have screws, carefully pry the sides apart with an X-Acto knife.

2 Use a pair of pliers to remove the guts of the cassette, including tape, posts, and cogs (B).

3 With clear electrical tape, create a hinge between the sides of the cassette by cutting a piece of tape the length of the long side of the cassette. Fold a seam in the tape and then affix the piece to the outside of the cassette (C). Cut another piece of tape and apply it to the inside of the case.

4 To prevent the case from opening on its own, affix the magnets inside the front edge of the case (D).

5 Fill the case with your business cards. Now you're ready to network like a rock star!

Male Chauvinist Tears Coffee Mug

We feminists can't help it if our forward-thinking, patriarchy-busting ways make sexists weep. Sweeten your coffee with male chauvinist tears—or at least pretend to—with this sarcastic coffee mug.

SUPPLIES

White ceramic coffee mug (glazed and finished; not an unfinished "paint your own" mug)

Pencil and paper

Oil-based paint markers

Rubbing alcohol and paper towels

Oven

Cookie sheet

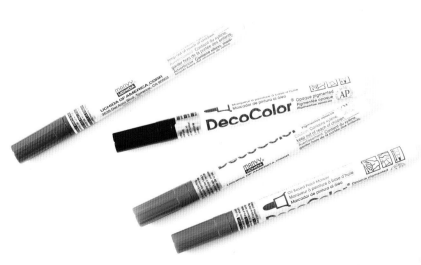

INSTRUCTIONS

1 Use the pencil to sketch out your slogan on a piece of paper. Then copy the letters onto the mug using a paint marker in the color of your choice. (If you make a mistake, scrub off the ink with a little rubbing alcohol and a paper towel.)

2 Draw teardrops onto the mug, according to your own design.

3 Let paint dry for a few hours or overnight. (This will help keep the design from wearing off with use.)

4 When paint is fully dry, preheat an oven to 425°F. Place the mug on a cookie sheet.

5 Bake mug for 20 minutes to set the paint. Let cool before using.

Oil-based paint markers are awesome for decorating ceramics and can be found in craft stores and online. Sharpie makes an excellent set—just be sure to use the Sharpie paint markers, not regular Sharpies.

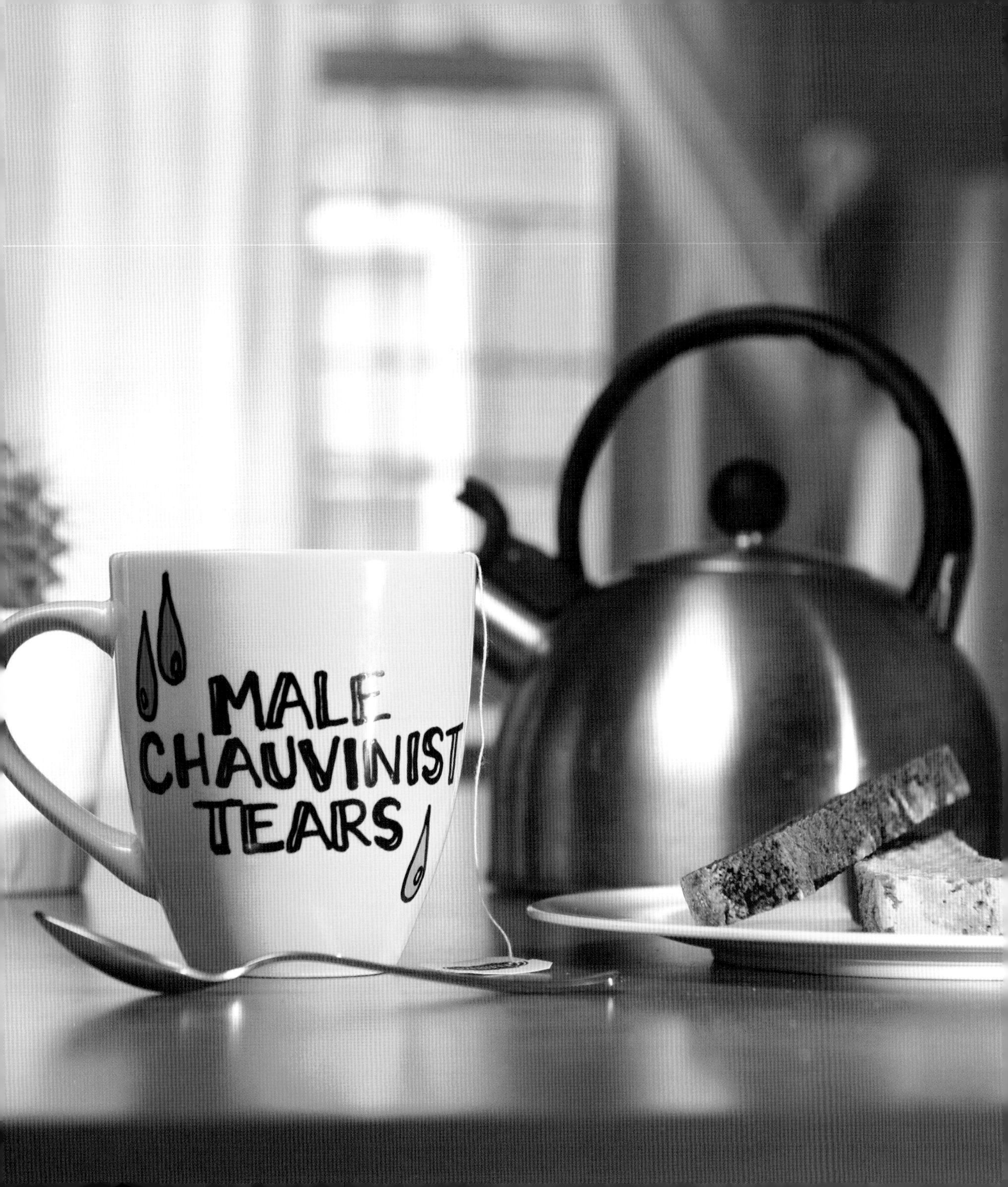
MALE
CHAUVINIST
TEARS

Food for Thought Plates

These food-safe decoupaged plates make whimsical kitchen art as well as the perfect platform for a snack. (They are not dishwasher safe, so clean them by hand.) Look online for vintage or copyright-free images of foods and people cooking and eating, and snip art and lettering from take-out menus and magazines that can spell out a tasty slogan.

SUPPLIES

Take-out menus

Copyright-free illustrations

Magazines

Scissors

Clear glass plates

Mod Podge

Paintbrushes and paper plate

Origami paper

Hammer, nails, and spring-loaded
   plate hanger (for wall-mounting, optional;
   see tip on page 96)

INSTRUCTIONS

1 Cut out all pictures and letters or words.

2 With a paintbrush, apply Mod Podge to the front of your center image (A) and adhere the image to the back of the plate so that it shows through the front. Brush the back of the image with additional Mod Podge to seal it in place.

3 Repeat step 2 with the other cutouts.

4 Cut out a circle of origami paper (or several pieces) large enough to fit over the back of the plate. Brush Mod Podge onto the patterned side of the paper and press to adhere it to the back of the plate (B). The paper's pattern or color should show through the plate. Brush the back of the paper with more Mod Podge. Let dry.

> **TIP:** To hang your plate, hammer a nail into the wall on which you want to display the plate. Attach the plate to a spring-loaded hanger and hang it on the wall. To use the plate for foods, choose relatively tidy items (think cheese and crackers, not lasagna). Clean the top only with a damp soapy cloth.

TASTY SLOGANS FOR YOUR PLATES

Make Your Own Dinner

Riots Not Diets

Sushi Rolls, Not Gender Roles

Cookin' Up a Revolution

Kiss My Grits

One Tough Cookie

Treat Yo' Self!

Not Your Cupcake

CRAFT FOR CHANGE

Crafting for yourself can be a blast, but crafting to help other people? Amazing. Here are ways to do good with your DIYs.

SOLICIT SPONSORSHIPS

Make a bunch of cute "adoptables" (try the Heroes of Feminism Finger Puppets, page 19, or Tampon Buddies, page 31) and post their pictures on social media, asking your friends and family to "sponsor" one. For a small donation to the feminist charity of your choice, you'll send your loved one a cute handmade friend!

TEACH YOUR CRAFT

Ask around to see if local after-school or adult education programs need volunteers, then lead a craft workshop. Pick a craft that's easy (so all crafters feel welcome) and cheap (so you can provide supplies yourself and the cost won't be prohibitive)—try Strong Female Character Prayer Candles (page 103) or Feminist Badges of Honor (page 15).

GO GUERRILLA

Hide—or proudly display!—your creations in public places to get your message across. Or see if a local coffee shop will hang your Food for Thought Plates (page 95), Em-broad-ery Hoop Art (page 49), or Grrrl Coat of Arms Banner (page 99) on their walls. You can even offer them for sale and donate the proceeds to charity.

GIVE SOMETHING BACK

Shopping for supplies? Buy extra and donate them. When shopping for packs of panties (Power Panties, page 45), tampons (Tampon Buddies, page 31), or baby onesies (Next-Gen Feminist Onesie, page 85), pick up twice as many as you need and give the rest to a local women's shelter or food pantry—they're often *way* understocked on basics.

PUT OUT A TIP JAR

Throw a crafternoon party (see page 83 for how-tos) and ask every guest to bring a cash donation for a feminist charity. You can coordinate the craft to your cause: make Burning Bras (page 65) for breast cancer awareness, Vagina Tree Ornaments (page 59) for reproductive health, or Food for Thought Plates (page 95) for a local food pantry.

Grrrl Coat of Arms Banner

Just as the fortresses in *Game of Thrones* display banners featuring the crests of famous family houses, your own regal manor should have a coat of arms hanging from the rafters. Design a grrrl-power crest that shows off all your feminist interests, from reproductive rights to the women of NASA.

SUPPLIES

Large felt sheets (at least 36 inches square) in various bold colors plus white

Smaller felt sheets in multiple colors

Pen or pencil

Paper

Fabric glue

Long wooden dowel (approx. 24 inches long)

Yarn or ribbon for hanging

Sewing needle and thread

Self-adhesive fabric letters

Decorative trim (optional)

INSTRUCTIONS

1 Select or cut a large, wide rectangular piece of colored felt to use as the banner backdrop. (It shouldn't be wider than the dowel length.)

2 Design your crest: On a piece of paper, sketch a shield shape and whatever symbols best represent your grrrl power—martini glasses, guitars, video game characters, superheroes, the Venus symbol, etc. Most coats of arms have three or four symbols spaced equally over the shield, or the biggest symbol placed in the middle with two smaller symbols flanking the sides.

3 Using your sketch as a guide, cut out the symbols from different colors of felt and then glue together as necessary with fabric glue.

4 Make your shield: Pick a large piece of felt in a color that contrasts with the backdrop. Fold the felt in half lengthwise. With a pen or pencil, trace a half-shield shape so that you'll have a full symmetrical shield when unfolded. (Make sure that the unfolded shield will fit on your background banner!) Cut along the lines and unfold.

5 Position the shield in the center of the banner and affix with fabric glue. Arrange the symbols on the banner according to your sketch and then affix them with fabric glue.

6 Make up a slogan (or use one of ours, right) that best fits your personality, and place the words onto your shield sketch to figure out the letter spacing. Cut a rectangular piece of felt large enough to accommodate your slogan and fit above the top of the shield. Adhere the letters to the rectangular felt and then use fabric glue to affix the felt to the banner.

7 Cut several small strips of felt to use as loops to attach the banner to the dowel. Glue or sew the loops to the top of the banner and thread the dowel through (A). Let dry.

8 Glue decorative trim around the edges of your shield (optional).

9 Tie a length of colorful yarn to both ends of the dowel. Hang your new banner in a place of honor!

FANCY LATIN SLOGAN IDEAS

Puellae personant cithara melior = Girls play guitar better

Vivant viragines = Long live female troublemakers

Ave regina = All hail the queen

Cogito ergo innupta = I think, therefore I'm single

Feminae domi senatuque = Women in the house…and the Senate

Strong Female Character Prayer Candles

In times of need, look no further than your favorite fictional females to give you strength and courage. These candles pay tribute to the pantheon of some of television's best women characters and look pretty snazzy in your apartment to boot.

SUPPLIES

Prayer candles (find them in the grocery store or online)

Computer and printer

Scissors

Paintbrush

Mod Podge

INSTRUCTIONS

1 Search the Web for images of the female characters of your choice. Print images. (When printed, the head should be about 1½ inches square, depending on the size of the image on your candle. You may wish to resize your image to fit.) Cut out the head and neck from your chosen image so that the bottom of the neck matches the clothing on the candle image.

2 Use the paintbrush to apply Mod Podge to the back of your cut-out. Affix cut-out to the candle so that the head of your heroine covers the head on the candle image. Brush with additional Mod Podge to seal. Let dry.

TIP: Jazz up your candles with glitter glue and rhinestones if desired to give them extra pizzazz.

3 Repeat steps 1–2 for as many candles as you'd like to make.

FICTIONAL FEMINISTS TO CELEBRATE

Abbi and Ilana from *Broad City*

Denise from *Master of None*

Kaylee, Zoe, Inara, or River from *Firefly*

Olivia Pope from *Scandal*

Cookie Lyon from *Empire*

Murphy Brown

Lisa Simpson from *The Simpsons*

Michonne from *The Walking Dead*

Mindy Lahiri from *The Mindy Project*

Princess Leia from *Star Wars*

Leslie Knope from *Parks and Recreation*

Xena, Warrior Princess

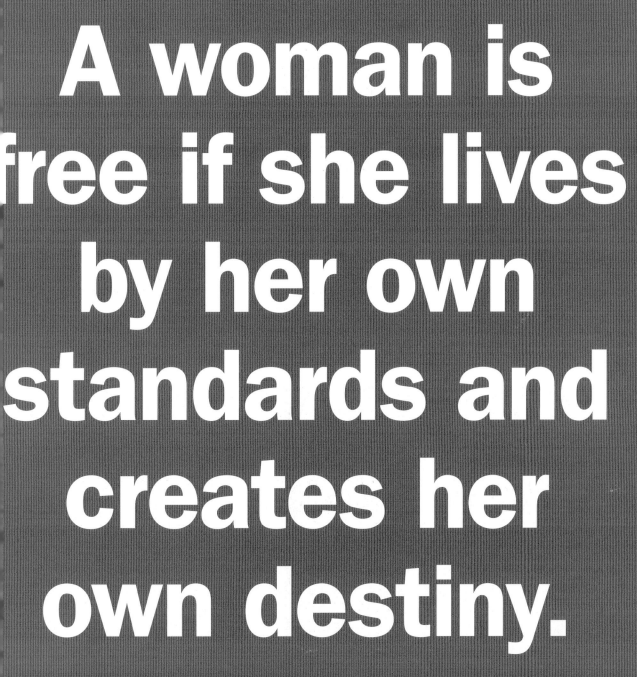

A woman is free if she lives by her own standards and creates her own destiny.

—Mary McLeod Bethune

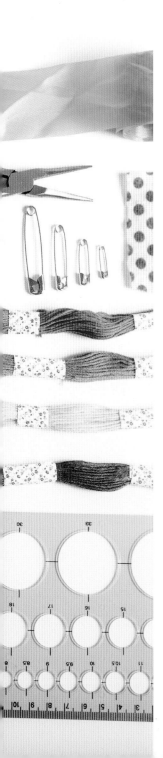

SUPPLIES

Crafting materials are easy to find when you know where to look. Your home—including the recycling bin—is probably chock-full of the things you'll need to make these projects. Craft stores (online and IRL) are another great resource for any tools or items you don't have on hand. For guidance on where to locate the good stuff, read on:

BEADS: Small beads, called seed beads, can be sewn onto fabric to add sparkle and sheen and to create designs. Buy them in a bundle of strands (called a hank) or by the ounce. Examine before purchasing to ensure beads are consistent in size and shape. Bigger beads are easier to work with but don't always lie flat.

BINDER CLIPS: These office supplies are perfect for securing felt and fabric after gluing.

BOTTLES, JARS, AND OTHER CONTAINERS: Consider using recyclables like glass bottles (make great vases), rinsed yogurt containers (perfect for mixing paint), and small jars or lidded coffee cans (ideal for storing small beads, buttons, glitter, googly eyes, and paints).

CHOPSTICKS: These utensils make handy paint mixers and glue spreaders; they also help to nudge polyester filling or fabric scraps into corners of stuffed dolls and pillows (page 41) and hold wicks in place while making homemade candles (page 69).

DRIED PASTA, RICE AND BEANS: For DIY mosaics, stock up on bags of dried legumes in various colors. Dried rice and pasta add texture and decoration to homemade art.

EMBROIDERY FLOSS: Embroidering—sewing colorful thread onto fabric to make a design—requires a special type of thread called floss, which is made of six strands. You only need two or three strands, so separate them before threading the needle: Cut the length of floss you'll need. Hold one strand firmly between your thumb and forefinger. With your other hand, gently pull away the rest of the floss, leaving a single strand.

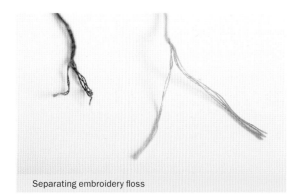
Separating embroidery floss

EMBROIDERY HOOPS: This circular frame of plastic or wood keeps fabric taut while embroidering. For most projects, the best hoop is the one whose size fits comfortably in your hand. Some projects may require small hoops or decorative hoops that become the frame in which the art is displayed.

FABRIC: Purchase textiles at fabric stores or online, or consider recycling material you already own. Give a stained sweatshirt or ripped pants new life as a puppet or throw pillow. Collect a variety of scraps in different materials (flat woven, stretchy knits, even single socks) to use for crafting projects.

FELT: Made by matting, condensing, and pressing fibers together, felt is cheap, plentiful, available in endless colors and styles, and easy to sew and glue. Felt made from wool and other animal fibers produces lovely results, but acrylic felt works fine for the projects in this book.

GLITTER: These tiny sparkly pieces come in any color you can imagine and in grain sizes varying from coarse to superfine. Grains of any size work for crafting; coarse glitter covers more surface area and therefore can be more economical. Note: no matter how well you clean up after a glitter project, some will *always* end up somewhere in your home (or on you!).

GLUE: For most of the projects in this book, basic craft glue (white glue or tacky glue) works best—it's water based and dries clear. Fabric glue can be useful. If you're in a glam mood, try glitter glue.

GOOGLY EYES: Adding these silly eyeballs to a puppet, doll, toy, or rock gives it instant personality. They come in all sizes, colors, some even with eyelashes! Self-adhesive varieties are convenient for quick crafting on the go.

HOT-GLUE GUN: An electric or battery-operated glue gun heats and melts cylinders of thermoplastic adhesive, which is then pushed through the tip of the gun when the trigger is pushed and resolidifies when cooled. There's almost nothing that hot glue can't bond, but be careful—it really is hot and can burn you!

MOD PODGE: The holy grail of decoupage—decorating objects with cut-out paper pieces—this medium with the groovy retro label is an all-in-one glue, sealer, and finish.

NEEDLES: Have these on hand for sewing and embroidering. When shopping for the projects in this book, don't let all the sizes and varieties of needles freak you out—pick something you're comfortable with. Helpful tip: embroidery needles have a bigger eye that accommodates thick embroidery floss.

NEWSPAPER: Before starting projects, lay newsprint on work surfaces to collect glitter, glue globs, paint splatter, and miscellaneous messes. Secure it with a circle of drafting tape between the table and the newspaper.

NOTEBOOK: Have a notebook handy to jot down crafty ideas that come to you while working on a project, or note important measurements so that you only have to cut once.

PAINT: All-purpose acrylic paints work for almost every craft and can be mixed to create custom colors. Always test a tiny area of the material you plan to decorate to ensure the paint won't damage the surface and appears as intended—when in doubt, check the product label. Puffy paints (which come in bottles with fine tips) are great for writing phrases on fabric.

PAINTBRUSHES: Unless you plan on finger painting, paintbrushes are a must. Sponge brushes or inexpensive synthetic-bristle brushes typically work fine. For larger decoupage projects, you may want a broader brush of about ¾ inches. Wash brushes with soap and water after use.

PENCILS AND MARKERS: Colored pencils and markers are decoration workhorses. Fabric pencils and water-soluble markers are perfect for tracing on craft materials. Chalk pencils (or tailor's chalk) make easy work of tracing designs on fabric. For doodling on ceramics, pick up oil-based paint markers.

PIPE CLEANERS: These colorful wire pieces you may remember from your childhood are ideal for making puppet and toy arms extra bendy.

POLY STUFFING: This common polyester filler is essential for making pillows fluffy, adding bulk to toys, dolls, and puppets, and giving extra cushion to quilts and blankets.

ROTARY CUTTER: A crafter's version of a pizza cutter, this rolling-blade tool is useful for cutting identical shapes at once from several pieces of fabric. For perfectly straight edges, place fabric on a cutting mat and then roll rotary cutter along a ruler.

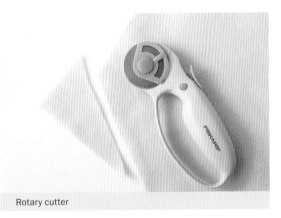

Rotary cutter

SCISSORS: Invest in three pairs—one specifically for paper, one for fabric, and one hardy all-purpose pair for everything else (e.g., tough cardboard or pipe cleaners). As long as you use each pair for only one material, the blades should stay sharp for a long time, but if you need to sharpen scissors quickly, use them to cut aluminum foil. Experiment with pinking shears, whose serrated blades prevent threads from unraveling and leave a fun zigzag edge.

SELF-HEALING CUTTING MAT: This work surface is perfect when using an X-Acto knife or rotary

GET STARTED STITCHING: A QUICK SEWING PRIMER

Never wielded a needle before? Have no fear! All sewing crafts in this book can be done by hand with a simple *running stitch*.

Thread a needle and knot the ends together. Hold the material in one hand and poke the needle through from the underside. Pull needle through until the knot hits the fabric. Make a stitch to the left or right of where the needle came through—no bigger than an eighth of an inch or so—then bring the needle back up. Repeat until you've sewn the whole seam.

If you want to add flair to a doll or finger puppet, sew the edges with a *whipstitch*, wrapping the thread around the fabric's edges.

running stitch

whipstitch

cutter on fabric or paper. Because the mat is made of a self-healing compound, any slices will close quickly.

SEQUINS: Sew these flat, shiny disks onto fabric for a flash of panache. As with glitter and beads, sequins come in every color of the rainbow. Although you can buy them already strung, loose sequins offer more flexibility; some projects work best using both.

SEWING KIT: Pick up one from a craft store or assemble your own. The perfect kit includes sewing needles of varying sizes, a pin cushion, straight pins, a seam ripper, and a thimble.

SEWING MACHINE: I like to hand-sew everything I make, but a sewing machine comes in handy if you're pressed for time or making multiples. You could go dizzy trying to figure out which style of machine is best, but at the very least you want one that makes the four basic stitches: straight stitch, zigzag stitch, button stitch, and backstitch. Features like automatic needle threading and touchscreens are nice but definitely not essential. Newer machines aren't necessarily better, either: a serviceable model inherited from Grandma will do. (Flea markets and garage sales are superb hunting grounds for vintage models; just make sure they work or are reparable.)

TAPE: Drafting or painter's tape is good for temporarily holding things in place. Stickier varieties like duct tape and fabric tape are better for permanent attaching. Use decorative styles like Japanese washi tape to up the fun factor of any cute craft.

TAPE MEASURE AND RULER: Rulers do more than measure—they can also help make a straight edge when cutting or tracing. A flexible tape measure is great for measuring supplies like fabric, wood, paper, or other unconventional materials, not to mention taking your body measurements for apparel. To help achieve a perfect angle every time, brace a T-square (a rule with a plastic head attached at one end) against the edge of a table.

THREAD: Basic sewing thread in a variety of colors is all you need for most of the sewing crafts in this book. Cotton thread works best with cotton, linen, and rayon fabrics; polyester thread is an all-purpose option suitable for most materials. Embroidery and cross-stitch projects require thicker multistrand thread called embroidery floss (see page 107).

X-ACTO KNIFE: This utility knife is ideal for precision cutting. The blades are interchangeable to suit different projects. Use a ruler as a guide and a cutting mat to protect tabletops and work surfaces.

YARN: Spun from fibers into a continuous length, yarn can be made from anything from cotton to polyester to wool to fuzzy alpaca hair. Standard cotton or acrylic yarn is perfect for the projects in this book.

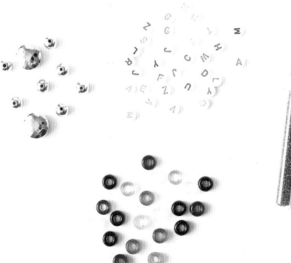

ACKNOWLEDGMENTS

Because it's very hard to make a craft book and stay sane at the same time, I have a few folks to thank for making this book possible.

To my mom, who always told me to be myself and stand my ground.

To my literary agent Bree Ogden, who helped make this book possible. Because of her, this whole book business so much more fun. Best partner in crime ever.

To my book editor Blair Thornburgh, for being the kind of editor I always dream of working with—patient, humorous, well-informed, full of great ideas, and a fellow feminist who doesn't look at me strange when I talk about sewing a huggable uterus pillow.

To my art director Andie Reid, for designing this book so it looks so freaking fantastic that no one can resist picking it up and giving it a gander.

To my book photographer and stylist Liz Daly, who came up with endless ideas on how to make these crazy crafts look perfect for anyone's home. Because of her I finally have a glamorous author photo of myself with a Ruth Bader Ginsburg finger puppet.

To my friend Felicia Day, who not only wrote a touching forward for this book, but also continues to be an inspiration to me in everything I try to accomplish. Plus she put me in her hilarious YouTube series "Vaginal Fantasy Book Club Show" where we drink too much wine and discuss paranormal romance books.

To my fellow gal pals who believe in me and this book: Anne Wheaton, Caroline Mizumoto, Veronica Belmont, Kiala Kazebee, Jenny Lawson, Sam Maggs, Jane Wiedlin, Jenna Busch, Laraine Newman, Kari Byron, Liz Smith, Gail Porter, Tracy Cannobbio, Meredith Salenger, Charlie Jane Anders, Annalee Newitz, Diva Zappa, Amber Benson, Kelly Sue DeConnick, Adrianne Curry, Sarah Kuhn, Lynn Bartsch, Jeri Ryan, Jennifer Landa, Cecil Castellucci, Amy Berg, Rileah Vanderbilt, Clare Grant, Hannah Hart, Kami Garcia, Jane Espenson, Janna Zagari, Stephanie Thorpe, Cat and Amanda Staggs, and so many more awesome ladies.

To the famous feminists who influenced me to make this book: Gloria Steinem, Emma Watson, Rachel Bloom, Caitlin Moran, Dorothy Parker, Shonda Rhimes, Margaret Cho, La Loca, Kathleen Hanna, Pussy Riot, Tina Fey, Amy Poehler, Ruth Bader Ginsburg, and the Suffragettes.

Special thanks to my craft buddy Ariel Fournier, who shakes up sassy cocktails so we can craft under the influence. Because of her I now know that glitter and champagne complement each other quite well.